FROM THE
HEART

RICK YEAGER

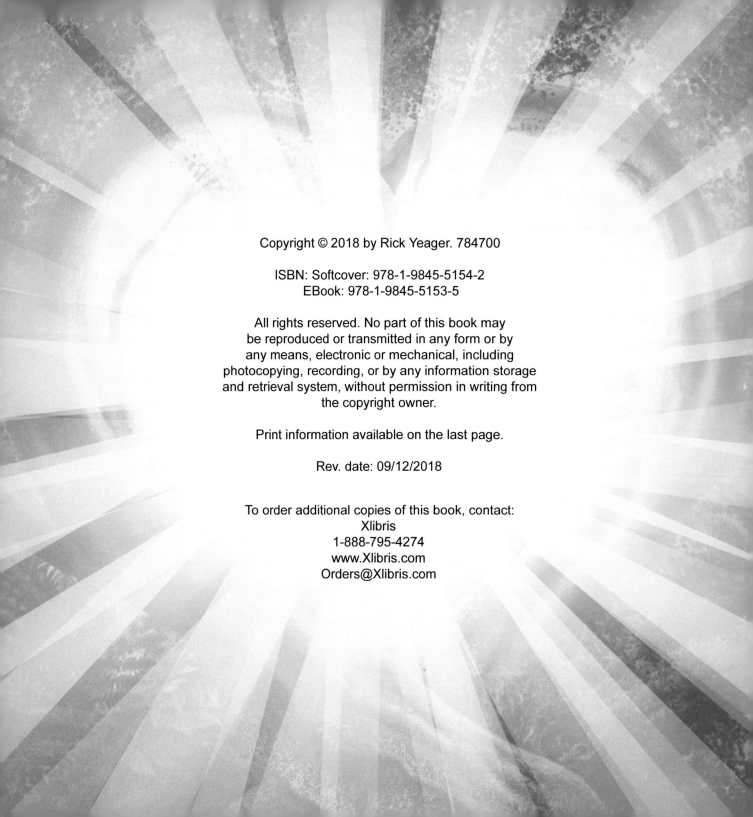

To order additional copies of this book, contact:
Xlibris
1-888-795-4274
www.Xlibris.com
Orders@Xlibris.com

In Loving Memory of My Donor Hero
Tommy Lamar Simmons

July 27, 1991-June 6, 2018

Tommy Lamar Simmons was born to Teresa Simmons and Tommy Lowe at The Med in Memphis, Tennessee. Tommy had four sisters; Jessica, Tiffany, Raychel and Regina: three brothers; Nathan, T.J., and Nick. Tommy has two children Penni and Liam who were his entire world. He loved his family dearly. Tommy grew up in Olive Branch, Mississippi with his mother and step-father Rodney. Tommy played baseball and was musically talented. Tommy played in the school band from the fifth grade through the twelfth grade and received a band scholarship to NCC in Senatobia, Mississippi. Tommy was very outgoing and never met a stranger. He always said "Your first impression may be your last, so make it count." Tommy worked as a manger for a restoration/moving company. He just recently started working on his own music. He wrote and recorded a song **"No Cuffin"** right before he passed away. Tommy's family and children meant everything to him. They will never forget the memories, laughs, and tears they all shared with him or the way he cared for all of them so very much. Tommy made sure his last impression would count, he will now live on forevermore, in our hearts, and in the lives of others that he never even met. Tommy was my organ donor who saved my life. I honor my hero in my last poem "The Gift of Life".

Wishing Upon a Star

As a child I looked to the sky to find a shining star
The biggest and brightest I could see would seem so far
I wish for things I wanted or dreamed
It was like I was speaking to the heavens
and God was there to listen to me
As I grew older I realized the stars had no means
I look toward heaven and spoke to the Man
The one who holds my life in the palms of his hands
I pray and I cry praying he will hear
This sickness I have, I'm beginning to fear
All levels of hope and faith prevails
What's in his plan only time can tell
For God is almighty and has his plans for me
I look toward heaven and pray and plead on my knees
That God will take care of my family and me
If it's God's will for me to be healed
He will make me complete and whole again
If it's not his will for me at this time
I know he will reach his hand out for mine
To take me to a place where there is no pain
There is forever sunshine and never a rain
When a child looks toward heaven and wishes upon a star
Someone in heaven is looking from afar
They are wishing for their hopes and their dreams to come true
By wishing upon a star

Somewhere Along the Way

Somewhere along the way I lost the man I am

Hepatic Encephalopathy has taken me to some unknown land

This Demon has stolen my sanity and made life a living hell

My family that's around me it's so easy for them to tell

I'm not the dad or Grandpa they loved so damn well

They shout out in anger, where's the man they once loved

We want you back in our lives the man we loved before

But somehow I lost myself along the way

I look into the mirror and ask who am I, what am I

Who is this demon that I have become staring back at me

And a voice in my reflection says he doesn't know anymore

For I lost myself somewhere along the way

One day the light will shine much brighter

I will return as the man I was once my battle is won

Somewhere along the way

If Tears Could Speak

Being ill with a life threatening disease makes you sad

You wonder why it's so tough and I get so mad

Not knowing what tomorrow may bring your way

Will there be another night or the light of day

Sometimes I feel so all alone and no matter how I try

It never seems to get better and sometimes I cry

I look toward Heaven and pray that a better day will be near

Sometimes I can speak to God through my tears

If tears could speak you would be amazed at what they would say

The broken soul that has heartaches and pain

No one knows the soul behind the tears how it hurts with despair

If tears could speak it would release your soul from all the pain

They say tears are a language only God understands seems so true

It can't be felt or understood by any other on earth

God gave us tears to release the pain and sorrow

If tears could speak our soul could be free

Hold My Hand

God please hold my hand along the way

As I walk this journey that's harder each day

The pain and the suffering it's getting harder on me

As you walk beside me, only you can see

The pain and the heartaches I feel each day

I need you to guide me along this difficult way

Give me strength and encouragement I pray dear Lord

To fight this battle with my shield and my sword

Let me conquer this disease and all its complications

When death is near and my strength has weakened

It's not my expectation to surrender or fall

I'll fight harder for my life and give it my all

I will fight to conquer no matter how big or small

I'm not giving in to death I'll stand proud and tall

on bended knees I will always pray

God hold my hand along the way

Make Me Whole Again

I used to be strong when I was young back then
Now I've become weaker, tired and struggling again
In my younger days there were few times of sickness
My body is like egg shells and ready to crumble
I'm feeling like humpty dumpty and my body shattering within
praying and hoping God will put me back together again.
God knows how much this old body can handle
Sometimes frustration sets in and I mumble under my breath
I start to have doubt and wonder if it will ever happen
I have faith in God and I believe God will heal this body
God will restore my body with a healthy liver and become whole
I may seem strong to my family and friends
You don't hear the prayers and the cries in the nights I fear
Many sleepless nights I lay awake thinking
What if this happens or what if I don't get well
Don't know how much more of this suffering I can take
When I go out in public with a smile on my face
No one can tell my smile and grin is fake
I pretend to be happy but my heart is so sad
In so much pain sometimes more than I have had
When it's time for my liver and I get the call
I know God will watch after me during it all
Guiding the surgeons with their knowledge and skills
God will provide me a second chance to continue my life
And put me back together again

My Battle Cry

I lay in bed each night and cry

I fight for my life I know may die

I won't give in to this horrible disease

I pray to Him on bended knees

To fight for my life one day at a time

Not knowing if tomorrow will be mine

I put on the armour of faith and hope

There are days this disease is hard to cope

The shield of strength I carry each day

The armour of hope I will always display

The courageous fight of this sickness I fight

Living each day as it may be my last night

Hear my battle cry I pray and I cry

Not knowing it may be my last and die

Give me the strength to carry on my life I plead

Knowing I have lived my life and helped others in need

Help me grow stronger to carry on

To fight the battle that may soon be gone

Let my light shine before others to light the way

To give them hope to be a warrior each day

Shed Your Light on Me

Dear God shine your light throughout this soul

Only you can make this sickly body whole

It will be in heaven where we never grow old

It's the beautifullest story I've ever been told

Angels all in white and bright as snow

Their soul and the halos are all a glow

The harps playing music we've never known

Bells will be ringing in the beautifullest tone

As I walked through heaven to meet you at your throne

I knew then you have called this angel home

The streets were all shimmering and shining with gold

It's a place much greater than I was ever told

As my soul walked near your great white throne

I knew my sickness was over and now I'm at home

My soul is no more worn, beaten down and torn

Today you gave me a new life and I was reborn

He Holds My Destiny

If my destiny is death, then it is my time to to say farewell
I'm prepared for heaven and not eternity in hell
So far this year has been a total hell being in and out of hospitals
My body and soul is deep in darkness and fail to escape
The pain that I feel, I'm ready to forsake
My time is ticking like a clock waiting for time to end
I'm just wishing my body will soon mend
The suffering while waiting for my second chance at life
is taking a toll on me
God, I want to be ready when the time comes to fight
Give me the power and strength to carry on
No matter how sick I will be in the end
As I fight such a hard battle so weak and tired
I believe in God as I fight that his blessings will prevail
As I reach for the mountain top climbing higher each day
At times it seems like all hope is gone
my life is like a puppet on a string
The doctors all controlling my fate as if I am not there at all
It's damn if I do and damn if I don't listen to their way
My body is saying he's tired and worn the hell out
It's time to get ready for my new chance of life
In God's time all this will be just a dream and become reality
That God will give me another chance at life

Life is Like a Candle

Life is like a candle shining so bright

When the wick is gone it's over

So keep your candle burning no matter where life takes you

Let your candle burn brighter each day

Because one day the wick will burn away

You will wish you had lived life to its fullest

Discouragement and disappointments will come your way

Protect the flame that burns within your soul

For one day life will be taken away

A candle burning at night is a beautiful thing

Knowing your soul will gain its wings

The life you have fought to win will take you away

Live each day if it were your last

Making sweet memories of the past

This you loved so deep in your heart

For someday our soul shall fly with the wind

Keep your candle burning each day and night

Life is too beautiful to give up the fight

Give it your all and push hard each day

Life's Pathway

As I walk down life's pathway
I look for a much brighter day
A day filled with laughter and smiles
Seems like a hundred thousand miles
I often wonder if today will be my last
Or if God will bless me with another day
My body is shattered and my spirits are low
I know God is able to help this old soul
I pray each night I will be given another day
Here on earth with my family to stay
I want to be happy and free from this pain
But in the end I know it's Heaven I'll gain
I trust in his word and believe in his power
I pray God give me many more hours
To spend with my family and friends
But I know it's time for this pain to end
Give me strength dear God to bear this pain
This disease has gotten me down and nothing to gain
I've been tested and tried many times during this journey of mine
Which road shall I take it's not up to me this time
Which path do I take, I ask each day
I get on my knees and begin to pray
That God will guide and set me free
And walk the path you have given to me

Tomorrow is Never Promised

I often lay in my bed praying there will be a tomorrow
Will I wake up with the sun shining through my window pane
Or hear the birds singing and chirping on the window sill
Or the sound of children playing outside and hear their laughter
I wonder if I will see my family again
Or watch my grandchildren playing together
The evening gatherings with family and friends
Will I miss their weddings, birthdays or graduations
So love them with all your heart and keep them within
For tomorrow is never promised for another to begin
Tomorrow is never promised so live your life each day
Be thankful to the Lord for each breath you take
For some there is no tomorrow, those who took their last breath
While struggling from a disease, a freak accident or by an act of violence taking their life
Be thankful for the little things such as the rain hitting your window
The sound of thunder booming loudly above
Be thankful for the stars and the moon and the night that's peaceful and quiet
The crickets and other sounds during the night
Be thankful for each day you are alive
Many lose their battle and take their last breath
For tomorrow's not promised to any of us
We fought the long battle and lived our life the best we could live
No more pain, suffering or heartaches
Because God has called our name

Just One More Moment

I stand at the door of death one day

Battling this disease has made me pray

It's getting harder on me more than anyone will ever know

My body is weak and can barely hold on

I wonder what life would be like without me

I would never get to feel my grandkids hugs or kisses

Or hear them say I love you

Or see them graduate or be there for their wedding day

I sit all alone remembering my life

Of all the great times I had with my family and friends

Knowing it could be my last on this earth

I ask God to give me just one more moment

Just one more moment with my family

To spend it happily with each once more

A moment to change any wrongs I may have done

To let them know I loved them so much

A moment to say I love you all so deep in my heart

It's a wonderful feeling and a pleasure to have you all in my life

I pray my memory will give you strength to carry on

To help guide you on your journey to make you so strong

Only A Memory Away

One day I will be just a memory
You may hear something I would say
Or hear one of my favorite songs
And our memories will take you away
To memories of the fun we made one day
Remembering the good times we all once had
With my son and my daughter
When we were happy or sad
All of the memories in our lives we made
Since you were very small kids
We laughed and we've cried many times
And wiped the tears from one another's eyes
There's a time to live and a time to die
When sickness steps in and takes our lives
The memories of our family we so loved
We hold deep within our hearts each day
So when it's my time to leave you
You can share our memories
I'll be one of God's angels in Heaven
Watching over you with pure white wings
When we meet again in Heaven
I'll be there waiting for you
At Heaven's door to welcome you
And memories of us will be in the past

My Letter to God

Dear God I come to you on bended knees

I lift my head toward Heaven and to you I plea

This sickness has been with me way too long

My body is weak and I'm not that strong

The waiting is getting the best of me

I don't know how much harder it could be

I'm weaker emotionally, physically and spiritually

I hide it from others and you can see

I pray each night to make me stronger each day

I need you Lord to help me along the way

Increase my courage and my strength I plea

I pour out my heart for a second chance you see

I know there is a reason for this sickness I bare

I put in my shield and my arm the warriors wear

I fight harder each day to stay positive and brave

I don't want to die and be buried in a grave

I have so much in my life I want to accomplish

You can perform miracles like feeding many with fish

You healed the sick and raised the dead

I ask that you make me whole and let my blood flow red

Heal this sick body oh Lord I pray

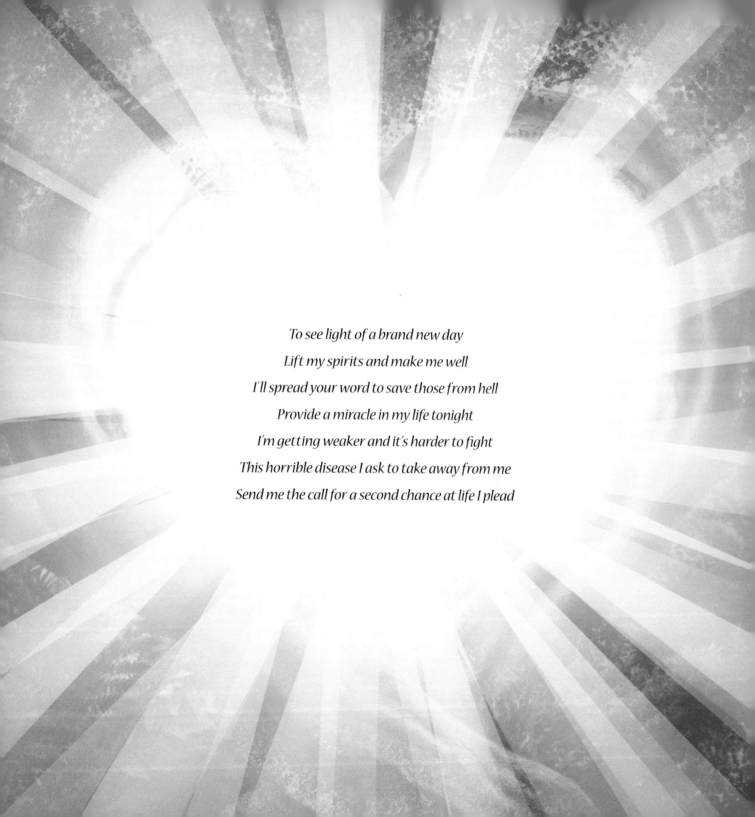

To see light of a brand new day

Lift my spirits and make me well

I'll spread your word to save those from hell

Provide a miracle in my life tonight

I'm getting weaker and it's harder to fight

This horrible disease I ask to take away from me

Send me the call for a second chance at life I plead

Shine Your Light On Me

Dear God shine your light throughout this soul

Only you can make this sickly body whole

It will be in Heaven where we never grow old

It's the most beautiful story I've ever been told

Angels all in white and bright as snow

Their soul and the halos are all a glow

The harps playing music we've never known

Bells will be ringing in the beautiful tone

As I walked through Heaven to meet you at your throne

I knew then you have called this angel home

The streets were all shimmering and shining with gold

It's a place much greater than I was ever told

As my soul walked near your great white throne

I knew my sickness was over and now I'm at home

My soul is no more worn, beaten down or torn

Today you gave me a new life and I was reborn

A Prayer from Us to You

Today I say a prayer for my Almighty God

Suffered enough, please get a new liver for his body

I'm a wonderful friend, dad and a grandpa too

Please send your loving angels to help me through

I deserve a second chance at life

Praying I no longer will have this strife

There's a lot of faith and prayers dear lord being said

That day is coming and I'm counting on you

They say I'm a great Warrior but I need your help

I silently pray as my head takes a bow

Tonight all my friends and family will pray

Please hear our cry and lift my spirit today

The time is here God to receive your power

We all pray throughout each hour

A donor be delivered for a new liver

I need that second chance now and not to quiver

I have faith dear God that my prayer will be answered

Right now I'm tired, weak and feel so numb

Please give me strength to be well again,

Through Jesus name we must now say, Amen

The Lord is My Shepherd

The Lord is my shepherd; I shall not want

He walks beside me through sickness and health

He maketh me to lie down in green pastures

He leadeth me beside the still waters

He guides me along this terrible journey I'm on

He will restore my health and soul

He leadeth me in the paths of righteousness for His name's sake

He will someday restore my health, my spirit and soul

He leadeth me along the path I must tread

Yea, though I walk through the valley of the shadow of death

I will fear no evil; for Thou art with me

Thy rod and Thy staff, they comfort me

When I'm close to death he will walk by my side

I shall never fear death at any time

He is leading me into the light at the end of the tunnel

I will not fear what lies ahead of me

He is my strength and guidance which comforts my soul

God preparest a table before me in the presence of my enemies

Thou anointest my head with oil; my cup runneth over

He is guiding and restoring peace within my soul

God is preparing me for strength to endure this pain

Surely goodness and mercy shall follow me all the days of my life

I will dwell in the house of the Lord for ever

I will have gained my reward for he was beside me each day

I will spend my life as a witness to others to help them along their way

For he is preparing me for a much brighter day

When You Are Dying

When you are dying with a terminal disease
The heart hurts deeply and my soul tries to please
The tears are always falling down my cheeks like a stream
One day I will wake up from this nightmare I scream
When I heard from the doctor and he told me so
I don't want to die young and my spirit is low
I held my head high and tried to be bold
My heart was breaking and my soul felt cold
The words without a transplant you can not survive
I pray each night that God will keep me alive
To watch my grandkids grow up with families of their own
For one day they will say I'm the best pops known
No one knows the hurt that I feel
Trying to mend a heart that's no longer steel
This sickness makes me respect the life I live
All of those special times which God can only give
I love each one of them in a very special way
And one day they can tell their kids he lead the way
With each of them we had our own special times
And know you hear an angel in the clinging of the chimes
For I have not left you but just stepped away
We will see one another on a very special day
So when you see the red bird flying so near
It's because I loved you so special and dear

Waiting on a Second Chance

Waiting on a second chance of life is the hardest part of a life threatening disease

When we were young we made mistakes and always asked for another chance

It's easy to say I'm sorry and then given a second chance

When fighting for your life waiting for a life saving transplant

You wonder if there will be a second chance for life

There's a shortage of donors and thousands on the waiting list to receive a second chance

Without a life saving donor we have no chance to survive

If I could save one life after I'm gone my life would be carried on

While waiting on a waiting list you become another number

And you become too sick to receive a life saving organ

Many don't survive the fight waiting and lose their battle

Please consider becoming an Organ Donor and give someone a second chance at life

What Hurts The Most

When you are dying with a terminal disease
The heart hurts deeply and my soul tries to please
The tears are always falling down the cheeks like a stream
One day I hope I will wake up from this nightmare that I scream
When I heard from the doctor when he told me so
I don't want to die young and my spirit is low
I'll hold my head high and try to be bold
My heart was breaking and my soul felt so
The words without a transplant you can not survive
I pray each night that God will keep me alive
To watch my grandkids grow up with families of their own
For one day they will say I'm the best pops known
No one knows the hurt that we feel
Trying to mend a heart that's no longer steel
This sickness makes you respect the life you live
All of those special times which God can only give
I love each one of them in a very special way
One day they can tell their kids he lead the way
With each of them we had our own special times
And now you can hear an angel in the sound of chimes
For I have not left you but just stepped away
We will see one another on a very special day
So when you see the red bird that's flying so near
It's because I loved you each so special and dear.

Organ Donors are Heroes

Hey there transplant patient
You don't know how blessed you are
You shouldn't spend your whole life wishing
Because something is bound to fall apart
Every time you're feeling empty
Thank your lucky stars
If you ever had an organ failing
You'd never want it to happen
You don't know how blessed you are
I've been on the road like the one you're on
You won't miss the sickness nor the pain
Because it is so damn hard
Take it from me transplant patient
You don't want to die and leave this life
I'm glad we talked this out cause it made me cry
You can have my organ to help you live on
Yours is in pieces and needs to be replaced
If you don't mind the scars or the pain
I'm an organ donor here to give you a better life
You can hang up your armor and end your fight
You may have my organ and start a brand new life
Without my organ donor my life would have been so short
You are my Heavenly Hero that cared so very much
You helped others live much longer and you live in our hearts
To give others the Gift of Life become an organ donor
You can save a life and and you will live onward

The Gift Of Life

You gave me Life when your life ended

You traveled this world and left so young

On the day the Lord called you away

You gave me life when mine was fading

We never knew our paths would cross one day

Your life was ending on this day

You became part of me and live on in me

I prayed for your family when you passed away

You gave me a gift that money can't buy

A stranger you left for me with great pride

You left behind family who loved you so dear

You entered heaven so bright and near

You became my hero in my time of need

When the Lord called you home

Even in death you left a great deed

Donating an organ to give life to me

You gave me a second chance at life

And now we live as one as days go by

You gave me life which is now a part of you

You're my hero which I never knew

Forever grateful for your unselfish act

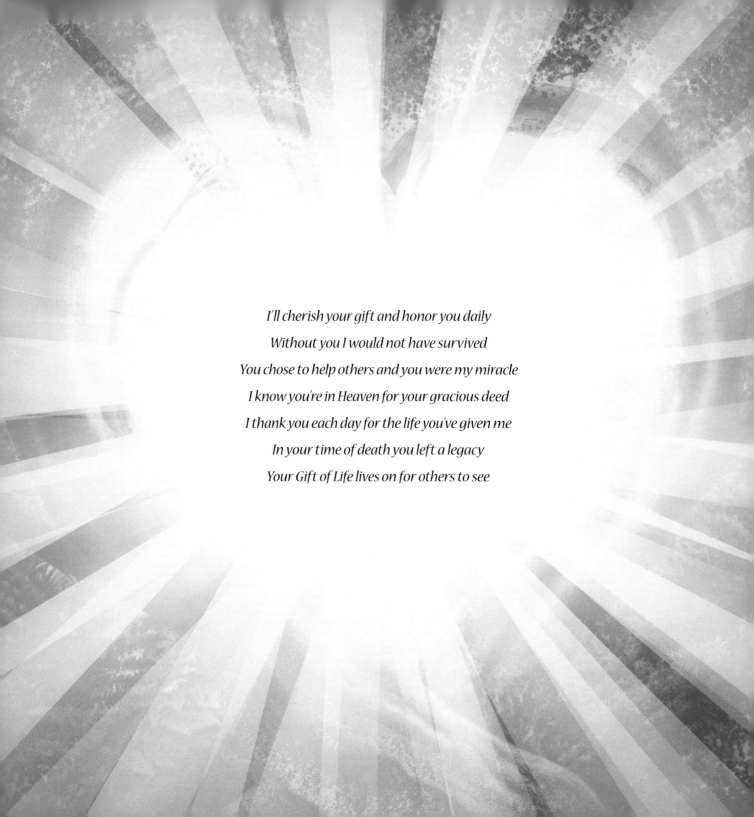

I'll cherish your gift and honor you daily

Without you I would not have survived

You chose to help others and you were my miracle

I know you're in Heaven for your gracious deed

I thank you each day for the life you've given me

In your time of death you left a legacy

Your Gift of Life lives on for others to see

Printed in the United States
By Bookmasters